THE **BOOK** OF

TIME
AND
SPACE

• • • • • • • • • • • •

Edited by Kate Tym

Published for
Tesco Stores Limited
by Brilliant Books Ltd
84-86 Regent Street
London W1R 6DD

First published 1998

Copyright © 1998 Brilliant Books Ltd
Printed by Cambus Litho Ltd, Scotland
Reproduction by Vision Reproductions

THE BOOK OF
TIME
AND
SPACE

• • • • • • • • • • • • • • •

Written by

Norris McWhirter

CONTENTS

HISTORY OF THE UNIVERSE

There are a few different theories about how the universe began, but most scientists agree that it probably all started with a Big Bang!

Scientists think that the universe was once just a tiny speck, packed with an incredible amount of energy. Then, about 18,000 million years ago, it exploded. The vast eruption caused a scattering of gases which, over time, formed into stars and planets. No one really knows how all this happened. Our understanding of time, energy and matter is of little use. There is still a lot that we don't know about our own galaxy, yet there are probably another 100 billion galaxies in the universe, each with 100 billion stars. What's more, the universe still seems to be growing! And it is very likely that there really are other life forms somewhere out there!

THE MYSTERY OF CREATION

The universe is about 18 gigayears (18 billion years) old, but the Earth is a relative newcomer, with an age of only 4.6 gigayears. So, if the life of the universe was squashed into a single year, starting with the Big Bang on 1 January, the Earth wouldn't appear until tea time on 29 September.

IN THE BEGINNING No one knows what caused the Big Bang (right), or what was out there before it happened. Many experts believe that it must have been God. Others are still searching for clues.

THE SOLAR SYSTEM

The Earth is one of nine planets that go round and round the star which we call the Sun. Earth is the third closest planet to the Sun after Mercury and Venus. The next closest is Mars. These four planets are known as the inner planets. They are all quite small and rocky with few, if any, moons.

After these four inner planets come Jupiter, Saturn, Uranus and Neptune – the four outer planets. They tend to have more moons and small rock cores surrounded by oceans of liquid gas. Last of all – near the edge of the solar system – comes the small, frozen planet of Pluto.

The planets emerge

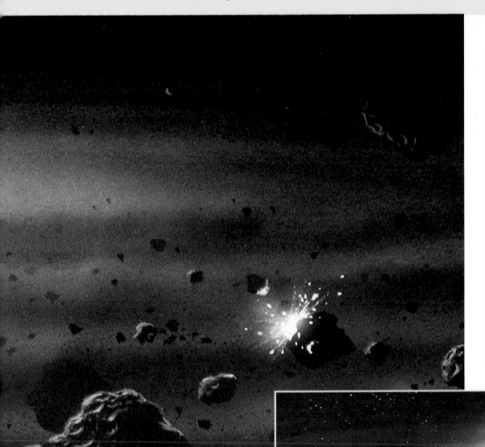

OUR SHINING STAR The Sun formed as a cloud of hydrogen gas and dust squeezed into a ball that heated up and began to shine 5,000 million years ago. About 300 million years later, a system of planets slowly began to form around the Sun, which is why we call our bit of space the 'solar system'.

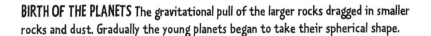

BIRTH OF THE PLANETS The gravitational pull of the larger rocks dragged in smaller rocks and dust. Gradually the young planets began to take their spherical shape.

THE SOLAR SYSTEM

Nine planets orbiting the Sun

All the planets orbit the Sun, but none of them travels in a perfect circle. They all orbit the Sun in an 'elliptical', or oval-shaped, path. This means that planets can sometimes be closer to us than at other times. So, when you're planning a trip to visit your favourite planet in the solar system, that's something you might want to bear in mind!

Between Mars and Jupiter, there is an asteroid belt, in which thousands of lumps of rock orbit the Sun together, in what looks like a great hazy band. In time they may start to form another planet.

Although the Sun is crucial to us, it is just one very ordinary star in our vast galaxy, which is sometimes called the Milky Way. The Milky Way contains about 100,000 million stars!

OUR GALAXY: THE MILKY WAY

FEELING SMALL It's hard to take in, but the whole solar system lies in just a small part of one of the Milky Way's spiral arms.

If you travelled at the speed of light, you could go round the Earth seven times in just one second. Yet, from the Earth to the centre of the Milky Way would take 30,000 years – even at 1,049 million km/h (670 million mph)!

THE SOLAR SYSTEM The lines show the planets' orbital paths around the bright Sun. You can see the asteroid belt between small, reddish Mars and Jupiter (bottom right).

11

THE SUN

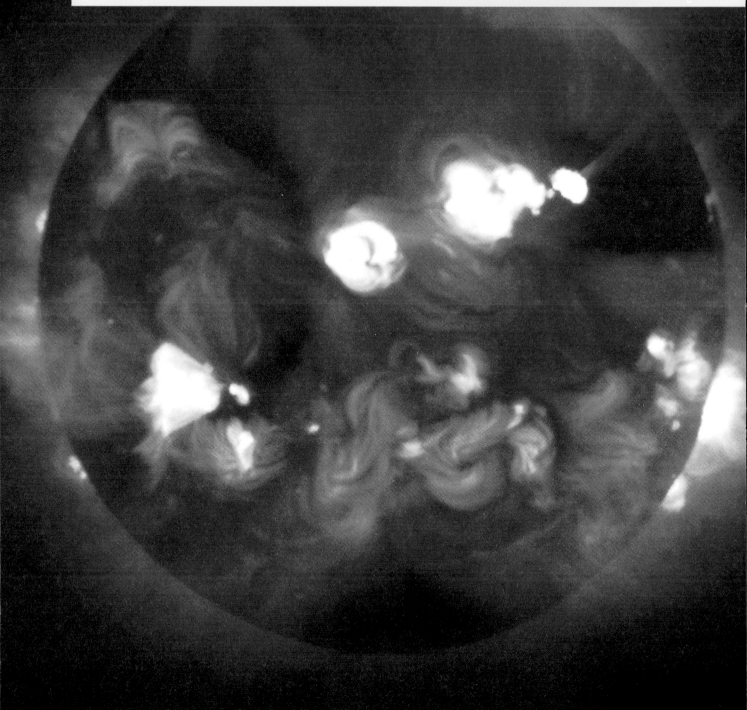

Our very special star

The Sun is a huge ball of burning gases at the heart of the solar system. It is about 1,000 times bigger than all the planets in the solar system put together. It is 150 million km (93 million miles) from the Earth. The Sun's surface is about 5,660°C (10,220°F), but at its centre, temperatures can rise to 14,500,000°C (26,100,000°F)! Its heat comes from nuclear fusion (the same process that makes H-bombs so powerful).

Stars shine at night, but the Sun, also a star, appears during the day! Though it's only an average star, it's very special to us. It provides all the heat and energy that living things on Earth need to survive.

Solar flares are violent outbursts of gas thrown up from the Sun's surface. They erupt, throwing off radioactive particles into space before subsiding again minutes later. The particles often interfere with radio waves on Earth.

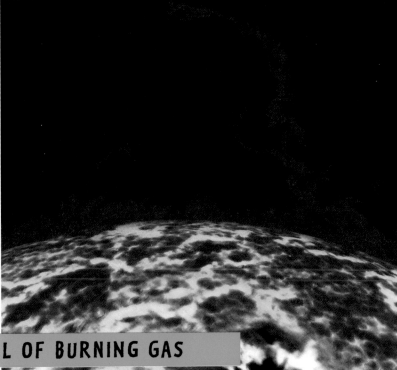

A GIGANTIC BALL OF BURNING GAS

SUN BURN The surface of the Sun is dotted with giant looping arches of burning hydrogen and helium, bursting out from the seething cauldron of heat.

THE SUN

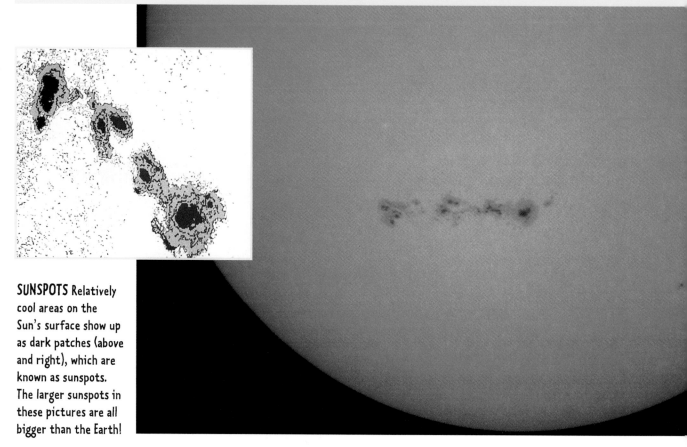

SUNSPOTS Relatively cool areas on the Sun's surface show up as dark patches (above and right), which are known as sunspots. The larger sunspots in these pictures are all bigger than the Earth!

The Sun suffers from spots – sunspots! These blotches are frequently seen on the surface of the Sun. They are actually areas of cooler gas which only appear darker, because they do not glow as brightly as the material around them. You could fit more than a million Earths into the Sun and most of the Sun's sunspots are larger than our entire planet!

Although the Sun is similar to many other stars, it seems much brighter and bigger to us than the all the rest, which we see twinkling in the night sky. This is simply because the Sun is many tens of thousands of times nearer to the Earth than the next nearest star.

Stars do not last for ever and once they have burnt up their supply of gas, they die. Luckily for us, the Sun has still got 5 billion years' worth of gas left!

Solar Eclipses

Every so often, the Moon passes between the Earth and the Sun, blocking part, or all, of the Sun from view. This is known as a partial or total solar eclipse. You can only see an eclipse from certain places – the next total eclipse in Britain will be visible from Cornwall on 11 August 1999.

TOTAL DARKNESS IN THE DAYTIME

SOLAR ECLIPSE As the Moon passes in front of the Sun, the Sun gradually disappears behind it and then reappears. The glow shown here is called the corona – the faint outer atmosphere of the Sun which looks like a pearly-white halo.

PLANETS
AND MOONS

The word 'planet' comes from the Greek verb 'to wander'. This is because when ancient astronomers first spotted five of our planets, they thought they were five stars that wandered around the sky.

HEAVENLY BODIES The Earth is the only planet that isn't named after a Roman god. From left to right, are Mercury (the messenger), Venus (the goddess of love), the Earth, Mars (the god of war), mighty Jupiter (the ruler of all the gods), Saturn (the god of agriculture), Neptune (the god of the sea), Uranus (Saturn's father) and finally Pluto (the god of the underworld).

Planets are cosmic bodies that do not give out any light of their own. Stars glow, but planets shine only because they reflect the light of their parent stars. In our own solar system, the planets shine by reflecting light from the Sun.

All the planets, including Earth, spin round, with each revolution taking a 'day'. While they are spinning, they also orbit the Sun – it takes them a 'year' to go full circle round it. The planets that are closer to the Sun have shorter orbits than those that are further away. So some planets have much longer years than ours, while others have shorter ones. If you lived on Pluto, it would be 248 Earth years before you could celebrate your first birthday!

UNKNOWN PLANETS
Scientists believe that there could be millions of other planets orbiting other stars in the universe. Some might even be quite similar to Earth.

BLAST OFF!

If you want to check out the planets at close range, hop on board our rocket and blast across the universe at a speed of 54,614 km/h (33,956 mph) – that's the fastest a rocket has ever gone. Guess how long it will take you to get there – it may be longer than you think!

MERCURY

ercury, the planet closest to the Sun, is only visible soon after sunset or soon before sunrise. Keep an eye out for a bright pinkish star – it could be elusive Mercury! It is brighter than any of the stars in the whole sky.

Mercury is very small – it's about the size of our moon. Despite its size, however, it has some very big craters. One called Ictinus is 4.8km (3 miles) deep – which is equivalent to nearly half the height of Mount Everest.

Mercury's core is believed to be made of iron and the planet has a very thin layer of helium gas surrounding it.

• A false-colour radar map
• of Mercury (above)
• shows the extremes of
• temperature just below
• the planet's surface. The
• red on the left is caused
• by the intense heating of
• the nearby Sun.

EVENING APPEARANCE In this picture, taken just after sunset, Mercury is the lowest of the three tiny star-like objects.

The closest planet to the Sun

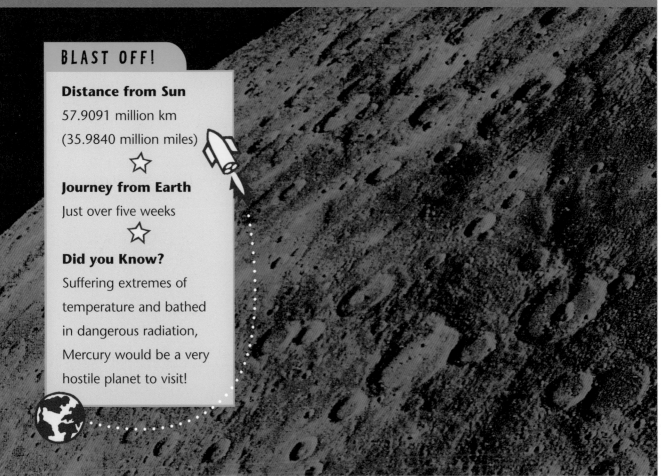

BLAST OFF!

Distance from Sun

57.9091 million km

(35.9840 million miles)

☆

Journey from Earth

Just over five weeks

☆

Did you Know?

Suffering extremes of temperature and bathed in dangerous radiation, Mercury would be a very hostile planet to visit!

Although Mercury is neither the hottest nor the coldest planet, it has a temperature range greater than any other – from 427°C (800°F) in the day, down to -180°C (-292°F) at night. That's six times

PITTED WITH CRATERS The first close views of Mercury were obtained by the US space probe Mariner 10, in 1974. They showed a surface remarkably like that of the Moon.

hotter than the hottest ever temperature on Earth, and more than seven times colder than a normal freezer.

Because of Mercury's oval-shaped, or elliptical, orbit, it can sometimes be the closest planet to the Earth.

VENUS

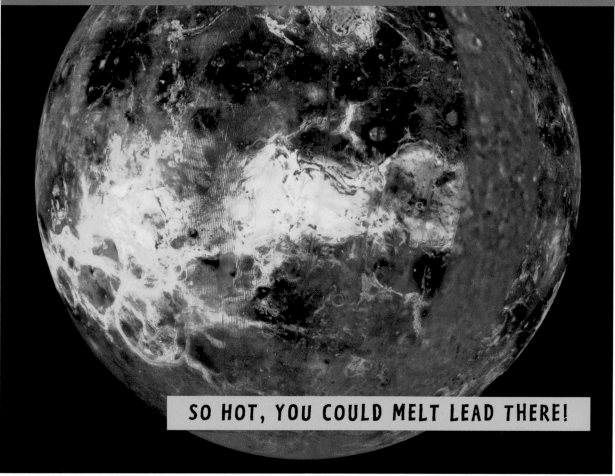

SO HOT, YOU COULD MELT LEAD THERE!

Venus is slightly smaller than the Earth, and it is the brightest and hottest of all the planets. The reason it's so hot is that it is permanently covered in clouds of poisonous gases, which trap the Sun's heat. The temperature on Venus can reach 462°C (864°F) – over six times hotter than our world record of 58°C (136°F) in Libya, North Africa, in 1922. And if that's not

THE EAST HEMISPHERE of Venus with the bright continent of Aphrodite Terra at its centre.

enough to put you off paying a visit to it, the pressure of the atmosphere is

The hottest of all the planets

90 times greater than the Earth's. So, you'd be roasted and squashed before you could see anything!

Venus is usually visible either in the eastern sky before sunrise or in the western sky after sunset. For that reason, it is sometimes called the morning star or the evening star – but, of course, it isn't a star, it's a planet.

Venus spins the opposite way to all the other planets, so that the Sun rises in the west and sets in the east!

- Venus is shrouded in dense clouds of sulphuric acid, which reflects the Sun's light, making it the most brilliant planet visible from Earth. Its atmosphere is made up of carbon dioxide.

VOLCANIC VENUS A computer-generated image of the Venusian landscape features Maat Mons – a giant smouldering volcano which is 5km (more than 3 miles) high.

BLAST OFF!

Distance from Sun
108.208 million km
(67 million miles)

☆

Journey from Earth
800 hours 16 minutes,
or 4 weeks, 5 days,
8 hours and 16 minutes

☆

Did you know?
It would be almost impossible for man to visit Venus because of its very high temperatures and thick, poisonous atmosphere.

EARTH

The Earth is the third planet from the Sun, at a distance of about 150 million km (93 million miles). Three-quarters of its surface is covered with water and it is surrounded by an atmosphere of gas. If you were to look down on the Earth from space, it would appear to be blue and white – the blue is water and the white is the clouds that move over its surface.

The Earth is the only place in the solar system known to support life. This seems to be because of its perfect

positioning in relation to the Sun. Any closer and it would be too hot, any further away and we'd all be frozen! And our atmosphere is unique in protecting us from the huge amounts of deadly radiation

VIEWED FROM AFAR This picture of the Earth was taken by a weather satellite from 35,800 km (22,246 miles) away.

which are given off by the Sun. The Earth's strong central gravitational pull also helps – it stops us all from falling off the surface!

However, as there are an estimated ten billion trillion stars, most of which probably have several planets each, it's extremely likely that there is some form of intelligent life on at least a few of them. So, UFOs and little green men might really exist after all!

'EARTH-RISE' FROM THE MOON

Pictures taken by the Apollo 11 spacecraft during the lunar mission of July 1969 show the Earth rising over the horizon of the Moon.

The planet on which we live

DID YOU KNOW?

Always over Africa
Satellites launched to cruise above the Earth at the same speed as the planet rotates, always appear in the same position above the Earth. This is known as being in a geostationary orbit.

THE MOON

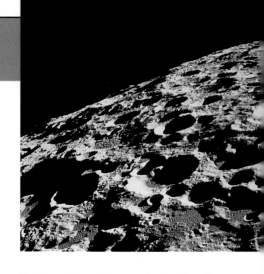

M ost planets are orbited by moons. The Earth has only one. It orbits the Earth, just as the Earth orbits the Sun. But instead of taking a whole year as the Earth does, it only takes about a month. Like the planets, the Moon doesn't produce light of its own, but reflects that of the Sun. As it goes round the Earth, the Moon always keeps the same side facing us, and it was not until space probes sent us images of the dark side of the Moon, that we knew what it looked like!

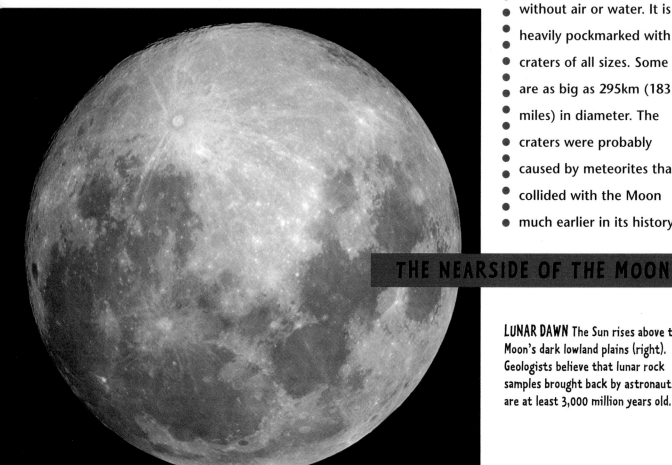

- The Moon is a rocky body without air or water. It is heavily pockmarked with craters of all sizes. Some are as big as 295km (183 miles) in diameter. The craters were probably caused by meteorites that collided with the Moon much earlier in its history.

THE NEARSIDE OF THE MOON

LUNAR DAWN The Sun rises above the Moon's dark lowland plains (right). Geologists believe that lunar rock samples brought back by astronauts are at least 3,000 million years old.

Our neighbour in space

MARS

Mars is not the nearest planet to us, but it's the only one which we are likely to explore in the near future – perhaps as soon as the year 2015. The closest Mars gets to Earth is 56.2 million km (35 million miles), which is still almost 150 times further away from us than the Moon.

Mars' surface temperature is closer to that of the Earth than any other planet – an average of -28°C (-18°F) against earth's 15°C (59°F).

WATER PROOF Water may once have existed on Mars, but it is now frozen in the polar ice caps, which gradually recede and advance with the arrival of the Martian spring and autumn.

RED DESERTS AND A PINK SKY

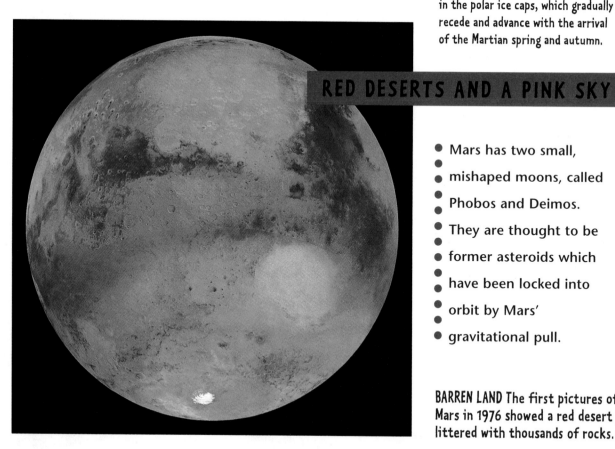

- Mars has two small, mishaped moons, called Phobos and Deimos. They are thought to be former asteroids which have been locked into orbit by Mars' gravitational pull.

BARREN LAND The first pictures of Mars in 1976 showed a red desert littered with thousands of rocks.

The red planet

MARS

Several space probes have visited Mars and have found that 'the red planet' is covered with craters. Some of them were probably formed by meteorites, while others are in fact volcanoes. Some of these volcanoes are the biggest in the solar system, but if Martian gravity was as strong as the Earth's, they would collapse!

DEEP VALLEYS Mars has a network of valleys which stretch almost a quarter of the way around the planet.

MOUNT OLYMPUS The largest known volcano in the solar system is Mars' Olympus Mons at 27km (17 miles) high – about three times the height of Mount Everest!

BLAST OFF!

Distance from Sun

227 million km
(141 million miles)

Journey from Earth

6 weeks, 3 days,
7 hours and 22 minutes

Surface temperature

Between -133°C (-207°F)
and 22°C (72°F)

Did you know?

Despite numerous attempts to find life on Mars, there are no signs of any Martians or anything living at all!

JUPITER

- We don't really know
- what Jupiter's surface
- looks like, since it's
- always shrouded by
- swirling clouds of gas.
- It could be made up of
- liquid hydrogen, while
- scientists think that the
- core of the planet may
- be made of hydrogen
- compressed into metal.

JUPITER HAS AT LEAST 16 MOONS

The fifth planet from the Sun and the largest of all is Jupiter. The Earth would fit into it 1,318 times over, and even its Great Red Spot is twice the width of the Earth. Although Jupiter is nearly five times further away from the Sun than the Earth is, it is usually still the second brightest planet. With a pair of binoculars, you can sometimes see up to four of Jupiter's largest moons. Of the nine planets in our solar system, Jupiter spins much

MANY MOONS Jupiter (top) is shown with four of its moons: Io (far left), Europa (centre), Ganymede (bottom left) and Callisto (right foreground).

more quickly than any other. It rotates at an extraordinary 45,500 km/h (28,300 mph),

JUPITER

as against the Earth's mere 1,670km/h (1,037mph). This is so quick that it actually causes the planet's equator to bulge, so that Jupiter looks like a squashed ball. Jupiter takes less than 10 hours to turn full circle, compared with Earth's 24-hour day.

RED ALERT The only permanent feature in Jupiter's atmosphere is the Great Red Spot (below). It is thought to be a huge storm that rages continually. The Earth is shown to scale (below right).

BLAST OFF!

Distance from Sun
778.3 million km
(483.4 million miles)
☆

Journey from Earth
15 months
☆

Surface temperature
-150°C (-238°F)
☆

Did you know?
Jupiter consists largely of gas and it doesn't have a solid surface – so landing a rocket could be tricky!

SATURN

The great ringed planet of Saturn is almost twice as far from the Earth as Jupiter. It would take about two years in a rocket, speeding at nearly 14.4km (9 miles) per second, to reach it. Saturn orbits the Sun at a distance of 1,429 million km (888 million miles).

MANY MOONS This image – made from pictures taken by the space probe Voyager 1 – shows Saturn and six of its moons. Saturn's largest moon, Titan (in the foreground), is as big as Mercury.

31

SATURN

Saturn is more than 95 times more massive than the Earth and has seven rings, which are not solid, but formed mainly of water, ice and rock fragments. The rings cannot be seen with the naked eye. The astronomer Galileo (1564-1642) was the first to spot them with his telescope. Up until 1898, Saturn was thought to have nine moons. But more recently, the space probes, Pioneer 11 and Voyagers 1 and 2, were sent to take pictures of Saturn, and the photographs proved that the planet had more than 20 moons!

RINGSIDE VIEW This coloured image from the Hubble space telescope shows Saturn's magnificent rings – one of the most impressive sights in space.

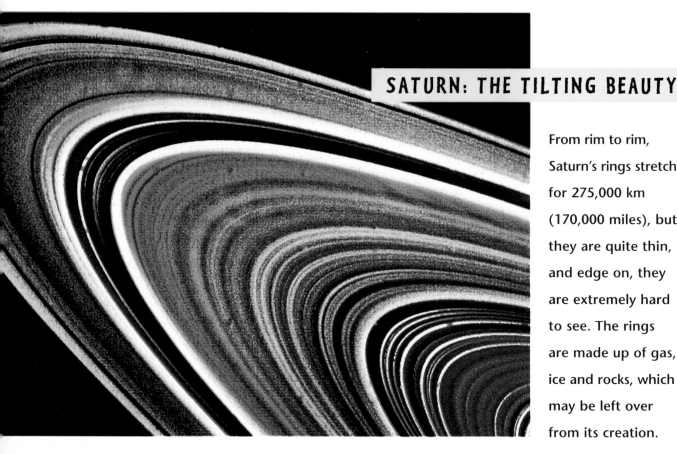

SATURN: THE TILTING BEAUTY

From rim to rim, Saturn's rings stretch for 275,000 km (170,000 miles), but they are quite thin, and edge on, they are extremely hard to see. The rings are made up of gas, ice and rocks, which may be left over from its creation.

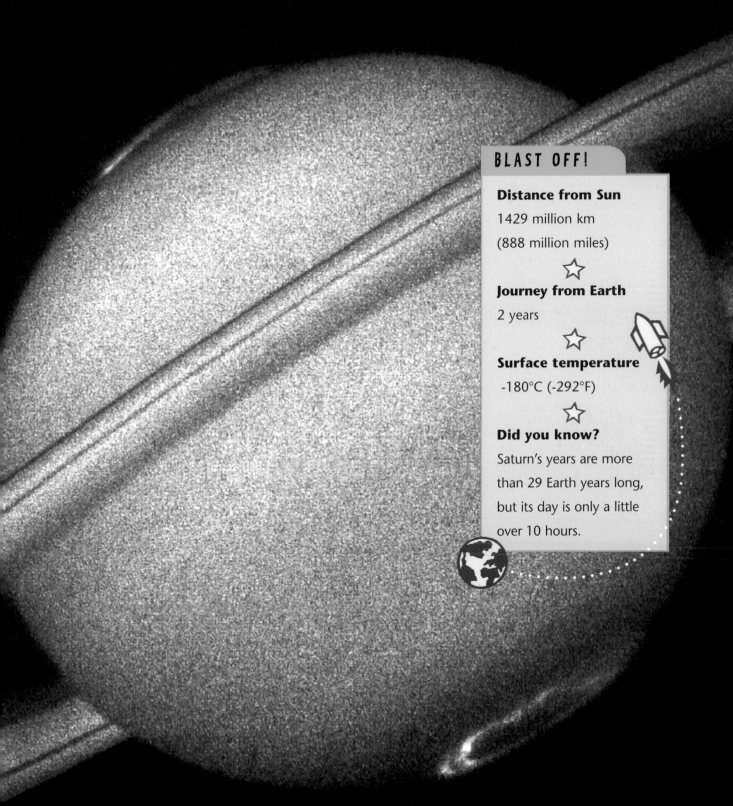

BLAST OFF!

Distance from Sun
1429 million km
(888 million miles)

☆

Journey from Earth
2 years

☆

Surface temperature
-180°C (-292°F)

☆

Did you know?
Saturn's years are more
than 29 Earth years long,
but its day is only a little
over 10 hours.

URANUS

The seventh planet, Uranus, was the first to be discovered after the invention of the telescope – 210 years later! Just visible with the naked eye, it wasn't recognised as a planet until 13 March 1781. William Herschel (1738-1822) was peering at the group of stars known as 'Gemini' with a telescope, when he realised that one of the stars he was looking at wasn't a star at all!

MOONLIGHTING Uranus (in the centre) is seen here surrounded by five of its moons which are: (clockwise from bottom, left) Ariel, Umbriel, Oberon, Titania and Miranda. In 1986, pictures from the satellite probe Voyager showed that Uranus has 15 moons in all.

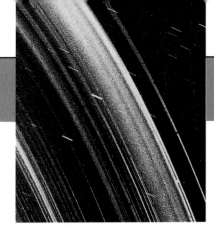

Topsy-turvy planet

RING CYCLE A telescope, carried in a C-141 aircraft flying at an altitude of 12.5km (7.7 miles), showed that Uranus possesses a system of rings like Saturn.

Uranus is a gas ball about 51,000km (31,700 miles) in diameter – making it about 67 times the size of the Earth. It is roughly 15 times heavier than Earth and has an ice-coated rocky core, covered in a blanket of hydrogen, helium and methane gas, which makes Uranus look slightly greenish from the Earth. Like Saturn, it also has several rings, which are probably made up of rock fragments.

Uranus orbits the Sun on its side, which means either its northern or southern hemisphere faces the Sun and receives almost constant sunlight, while the other remains in darkness. This creates very long seasons – summers and winters are about 21 years long!

BLAST OFF!

Distance from Sun

2875.04 million km
(1786.51 million miles)

Journey from Earth

5 years, 8 months

Surface temperature

-210°C (-346°F)

Did you know?

Uranus has a day which lasts for about 17 hours, but its year lasts for 84 Earth years.

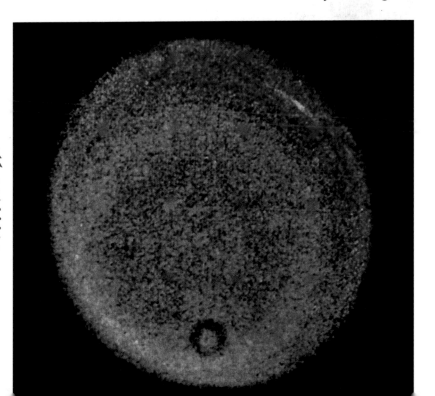

NEPTUNE

MOONSHINE Neptune has at least eight moons. This picture was taken from one called Triton, which is smaller than our moon and very cold.

NEPTUNE RISING OVER ITS MOON

The solar system's eighth planet was found by mathematics rather than by a telescope. In 1834, the Reverend TJ Hussey, who was the rector of Hayes in south-east London, noted that Uranus was adrift from its predicted position. He guessed that this might be due to the gravitational pull of another even more remote, unknown, planet. And in 1846, two astronomers in Berlin, Germany – Johann Galle and Heinrich D'Arrest – spotted a tiny disc, which was the eighth planet. It was later named Neptune.

Neptune is 57 times larger than the Earth and is the windiest planet in the solar system. Its bluish atmosphere – caused by methane – was photographed by Voyager 2 in 1989. The pictures showed some markings, including a dark spot – a violent spinning storm cloud which was at least as large as the Earth.

- Neptune has a very elongated, or elliptical, orbit around the Sun. So, up until the year 2,000, Neptune is further from the Earth than Pluto, which is usually the most distant planet.

UNEXPECTED DISCOVERY Although we can't see them from Earth, Neptune has five rings, which were discovered by Voyager 2 in 1989.

The most distant gas planet

BLAST OFF!

Distance from Sun

4,497 million km

(2,795 million miles)

Journey from Earth

9 years

Surface temperature

-210°C

(-346°F)

Did you know?

Winds can reach 2,160km/h (1,340mph) on Neptune, which is why its surface features change so quickly.

PLUTO

For 84 years, Neptune remained the eighth and most remote known planet of the solar system. Searches for an even more remote planet began as early as 1877 in the United States, but nothing was found until 23 January 1930. Working at the Observatory at Flagstaff, Arizona, USA, the 23-year-old, Clyde Tombaugh, discovered a very faint but moving image, close to the star Delta Geminorum. It proved to be the long elusive ninth planet and was named Pluto. With a diameter of only 2,320km (1,442 miles), it is the smallest planet in the solar system by quite some way.

SOLE IMAGE This blurred picture of Pluto, taken by the Hubble Space Telescope, is the only picture there is of Pluto and its large moon, Charon.

AN UNKNOWN, FROZEN WORLD

- Pluto is considered by some astronomers to be too small to qualify as a proper planet. It has a peculiar orbit, which takes it inside the path of Neptune for 20 years at a time. Some people argue that it could be an escaped moon or a satellite of Neptune, or even a large asteroid.

BLAST OFF!

Distance from Sun

5913.51 million km (3674.58 million miles)

☆

Journey from Earth

15 years there!
15 years back!

☆

Surface temperature

-220°C (-364°F)

☆

Did you know?

There are no planned space missions to Pluto. And the question of whether there are any more planets beyond it may remain unanswered for a very, very long time!

TIME

Time separates events from each other. For this reason, it can be regarded as the fourth dimension, to add to the three dimensions of length, breadth and height. We use the Earth's position in the universe to establish how we measure time.

Because the Earth is one of the nine planets that orbit the Sun, our nights, days, months and years are dictated by the warmth and light we get from that star.

Our planet, Earth, travels round the Sun in its own particular path. This path is called the Earth's orbit. At the same time, the Earth is spinning. It never stops spinning. If you think of an imaginary line running through the middle of the Earth from the South Pole to the North Pole, this is the line round which the Earth spins. It is called the Earth's axis.

The Sun shines all the time, but we can only see it if the side of the Earth we live on is facing it at the time. The Earth takes 24 hours to spin on its axis once – that's why a day always has 24 hours. And the Earth takes 365.25 days to complete a full circle round the Sun – which determines the length of our Earth year.

AS THE EARTH SPINS, DAYS AND NIGHTS COME AND GO

As if that's not enough to be getting on with, the Earth doesn't sit straight on its axis but is tilted over to one side. First one half and then the other, is tilted slightly towards the Sun. We call these two halves hemispheres – the southern hemisphere and the northern hemisphere. In Britain we have our summer from June to August – that's when our northern hemisphere is tilting towards the Sun. In winter, the Earth is tilting away from the Sun, so we get less of its heat and light, making the days shorter and colder. But in New Zealand – on the other side of the world – summer is in December and winter is in July!

NIGHTFALL IN VANCOUVER Different parts of the Earth face the Sun at different times. While it's midday in London, it's still the middle of the night in Canada.

MAN'S EXPLORATION OF SPACE

For centuries, people have looked up at the sky and wondered just what is out there. As technology progressed, it became a dream to travel into space and explore the universe at closer quarters. Eventually, that dream became a reality.

The first time space was reached was in 1947 when the Americans sent up a two-stage rocket from White Sands, New Mexico, USA, to a height of 392km (243 miles). From then on, progress was rapid. Only 12 years later, in 1959, the Russian space probe, Luna II, hit the Moon, 384,400km (238,860 miles) away from the Earth. America's National Aeronautical and Space Administration (NASA) was determined not to be out-done, but the Russians beat them to it with the first human to be launched into space – Flight Major Yuri Gagarin. As the rocket moved into orbit, Gagarin shouted: "Po-ye-kho-li" – Russian for "Here we go!" – and just 89 minutes 20.4 seconds later, Vostok I had safely completed the first ever orbit of the Earth.

SPACE PIONEER On 12 April 1961, the Russian Yuri Gagarin (above, left) became the first person to go into space.

EXPLORATION OF SPACE

Gagarin smashed every record in the book – going up to a height of 327km (203 miles) above the Earth's surface and travelling at a speed of up to 28,260km/h (17,560mph). But the most famous event in the history of space travel occurred on 21 July 1969, when Neil Armstrong became the first man to set foot on the surface of the Moon. As he stepped out of Apollo 11, his words were heard by a massive TV audience: "That's one small step for a man, one giant leap for mankind".

THE LAST MAN ON THE MOON Nobody has set foot on the Moon since the American astronaut Eugene Cernan, of the Apollo 17 mission, left it – as long ago as 1972.

Those famous footprints left behind by the first astronauts will still be visible in 10 million years' time! The reason is simple – there's no rain or wind on the Moon to wash them away!

...ONE GIANT LEAP FOR MANKIND

LIFT OFF! The Space Shuttle Challenger takes off from Cape Canaveral, Florida, USA. Tragically, it exploded in 1986.

We have lift off!

LOST IN SPACE

Along with the huge numbers of planets and stars contained in the universe, there are many other weird and wonderful objects drifting around in the vastness of space.

Asteroids are rubble – left over from the formation of the solar system. They consist of lumps of rock and metal – similar materials to those which make up the Earth, Mercury, Venus and Mars. Asteroids come in many shapes and sizes. The

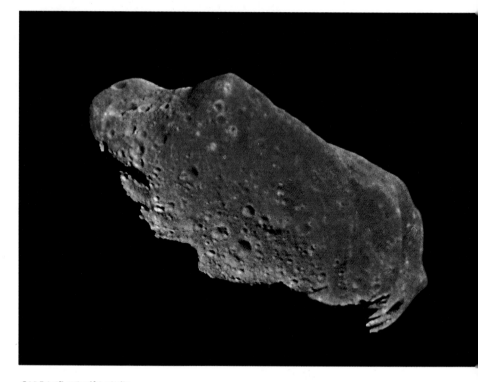

GARBAGE OF THE SKIES The surface of this asteroid, known as Ida, is pitted with craters, caused by countless collisions with rocks and other cosmic debris.

CELESTIAL FIREWORK Halley's Comet – made up of frozen gas, rocks and dust – was photographed by the Giotto spacecraft in March 1986. It won't pass Earth again until the year 2061!

A REGULAR VISITOR – EVERY 76 YEARS

first was discovered in 1801 and called Ceres. It is about the size of France and orbits the Sun every 4.6 years.

Comets are lumps of rock and dust, trapped in the ice of frozen gas. They are sometimes called 'dirty snowballs' because that's exactly what they look like. Astronomers think that they may come from an unknown cloud of billions of comets, far beyond Pluto. For most of the time, comets are in the far reaches of the solar system and are extremely hard to see. Only when they approach the Sun, do they warm up and start to glow. As the frozen gas starts to melt, it streams away from the head of the comet to form a flowing tail which can be millions of kilometres or miles long. Until recently, comets were regarded as evil omens, but now we know when they might return and marvel at their appearance. There is one bright comet, called Halley's Comet, which passes Earth every 76 years. People have been spotting it for centuries and even William the Conqueror is known to have seen it in 1066. It last passed the Earth in 1986.

METEORS AND...

M eteors are tiny particles which orbit the Sun. We can only see them if they fall into the Earth's atmosphere and burn up. They then appear as streaks of light, racing across the night sky – they are often mistakenly called shooting stars. Surprisingly, a typical meteor is no bigger than a grain of sand and burns for less than a second!

Meteorites, on the other hand, are rocks that are so large they will not always burn up in the Earth's

CRASH LANDING In Arizona, USA, a meteorite, 79m (260ft) wide, made this crater which is 1.27km (0.8mile) across.

atmosphere. And they can be very destructive as they crash to Earth. In 1908, one exploded five miles above northern Siberia, destroying

...BLACK HOLES

an area of forest about the size of Greater London. The largest surviving fragment of any meteorite fell to Earth in prehistoric times. All 60 tonnes of it can still be seen in the huge crater it made a little way outside the town of Grootfontein, in Namibia.

LIKE A BOTTOMLESS DRAIN

Black holes are one of the strangest phenomena of deep space. They are the remains of huge stars (often five times bigger than the Sun) which have exploded. The centre of the star is squashed so tightly, that it develops extremely strong gravity (about a billion times greater than that on Earth), which then pulls in and crushes all the objects around it. Black holes even suck in light rays. That's how black holes got their name and also why they're totally impossible to see!

BLACK DEATH An artist's impression of a red giant star, nearing the end of its life (upper left), and a swirling black hole (right) starting to suck everything into it.

ACKNOWLEDGEMENTS

Science Photo Library: Cover, cover BR, p3 & 11CR & cover 2nd TL, p7, p8-9, p10-11L, p16 T, p13 & cover CL, p15, p14R, p14L, p18L, p18R, p24BL, p36TL, p39, p40, p47, p46

European Space Agency/Science Photo Library: P23 & p16C, p45R

Harvard College Observatory/Science Photo Library: P45TL & p2CR

Jisas/Lockheed/Science Photo Library: p12

Nasa/Science Photo Library: Cover, p16L, p16 2nd L, p17BL, p19, p20, p21, p22BL & TC, p24TR & cover BL, p25, p27, p26TR, p28BL, p28TR, p29, p30TR, p30BL, p31, p33 & p17C, p32BL, p34, p35BR & p17CR, p35TL, p37 & p17 2nd R & p2 TL, p38 & p17TR, p42BL, p42TR, p44R & cover TL, p36BR

Novosti/Science Photo Library: P41

US Geological Survey/Science Photo Library: P26BL & p16R

Telegraph Colour Library: p2TR & p43, cover background, cover 2nd BL and back cover R

Abreviations: T = Top; B = Bottom; L = Left; C = Centre; R = Right.

Picture research by Leila Miller

OTHER BOOKS IN THIS SERIES:

**The Book of Animals • The Body Book
The Book of Extremes**